A Ticket to
Russia

Tom Streissguth

🌿 Carolrhoda Books, Inc. / Minneapolis

Photo Acknowledgments

Photos, maps, and artworks are used courtesy of: Laura Westlund, pp. 1, 2-3, 4-5, 13, 25, 38; © Wolfgang Kaehler, pp. 4 (inset), 7, 9, 14 (left), 27, 31; © Chris Stowers/Panos Pictures, p. 6; © Dan Buettner, pp. 7 (inset), 8, 10, 11, 14 (top), 17 (bottom), 22 (top), 25, 40; John Erste, pp. 15, 21, 32, 33, 36-37; Jeff Greenberg, pp. 12-13, 16, 17 (top), 19, 30 (right); Brian Ney, pp. 12 (inset), 28 (left), 44; © Mary Ney, p. 14 (right); © Jean S. Buldain, pp. 14 (center), 30 (left); © Trip/D. Iusupov, p. 15; © Vladimir Pcholkin/FPG International, p. 18 (left); Steve Feinstein, pp. 18 (right), 26; Sovfoto/Eastfoto, pp. 20, 42; Reuters/Bettmann, pp. 21; © Jeremy Hartley/Panos Pictures, p. 22 (bottom); © Trip/D. MacDonald, p. 23; © Trevor Wood/Tony Stone Images, p. 24; © Frank S. Balthis, p. 28 (right); Sergej Schachowskoj, p. 29; Martha Swope © Time Inc., p. 34; © Cliff Hollenbeck/Tony Stone Images, p. 36; Reuters/Stringer/Archive Photos, p. 37; © Trip/V. Kolpakov, p. 39; Hollywood Book & Poster, p. 41; AP/Wide World Photos, p. 43. Cover photo of kids and their grandmother at a railway station © Trip/A. Kuznetsov.

Carolrhoda Books, Inc.
c/o The Lerner Publishing Group
241 First Avenue North
Minneapolis, Minnesota 55401 U.S.A.

Website address: www.lernerbooks.com

Library of Congress Cataloging-in-Publication Data

Streissguth, Thomas, 1958–
  Russia / by Tom Streissguth.
    p.   cm. — (A ticket to)
  Includes index.
  Summary: Examines the geography, history, economy, society, and culture of the Russian Federation, formerly part of the Soviet Union.
  ISBN 1-57505-126-5 (lib. bdg. : alk. paper)
  1. Russia (Federation)—Juvenile literature. [1. Russia (Federation)] I. Title. II. Series.

Manufactured in the United States of America
1 2 3 4 5 6 – JR – 02 01 00 99 98 97

Contents

Welcome! 4

Siberia Is Big 6

Steppe Outside 8

Splash! 10

On the Move 12

People 14

Home 16

New Nation 18

Jobs 20

Family 22

Food 24

ABCs 26

Celebrate! 28

School 30

Story Time 32

Ballet 34

Music 36

Sports and Fun 38

New Words 40

TV 42

New Words to Learn 44

New Words to Say 46

More Books to Read 47

New Words to Find 48

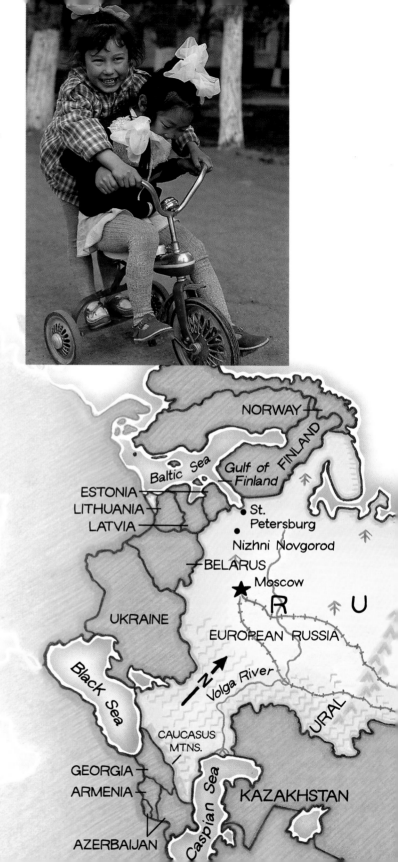

Hop on! Two girls try to ride the same tricycle.

Welcome!

Russia is easy to find on a map. Some people say Russia is shaped like a bear. But if you cannot find a bear, just look for the biggest country. Russia is so large it is part

4

of two **continents**—Asia and Europe.
The Ural Mountains form a border between
European Russia and **Asian Russia**.

mountains
taiga
tundra
steppes
★ capital

Alaska (U.S.)

Bering Sea

ARCTIC OCEAN

PACIFIC OCEAN

ASIAN RUSSIA

Yenisei River

Lena River

Miles
0   200   400   600
0   400   800
Kilometers

S   S   I   B   E   R   I   A

Ob River

MTNS.

S   S   I

Sakhalin Island

N

Lake Baikal

TRANS-SIBERIAN RAILROAD

CHINA

Vladivostok

Sea of Japan

5 JAPAN

MONGOLIA

NORTH KOREA

Siberia Is Big

The biggest part of
Russia is **Siberia.**
Siberia is so big that Russians need a few
days to cross it by train.

Siberia is part of Asian Russia. The
uppermost or far northern part of Siberia is
known as the **tundra.** The ground in the
tundra is always frozen. No trees can grow

there. Below the tundra is the **taiga**—a huge green forest. The taiga is the largest forest in the world!

Steppe Outside

Russia has forests and mountains and wide open fields called **steppes**. The steppes are not like the ones you walk up and down.

A river runs through a taiga forest.

Map Whiz Quiz

Take a look at the map on pages four and five. A map is a drawing or chart of a place. Trace the outline of Russia on a piece of paper. See if you can find the Baltic Sea. Mark this side of your map with a "W" for west. How about the Pacific Ocean? Mark this side with an "E" for east. Now color in the regions labeled European Russia and Asian Russia.

(Facing page) *Flowers bloom on the steppes in summer.*

In fact, they are just the opposite. These grassy fields are so flat you can see for miles around.

9

Hang on! A farmer hangs on while his son paddles their boat on the Volga River.

Splash!

Russia claims a lot of land—and a lot of water. Some of the country's waterways are famous. Lake Baikal, in southern Siberia, is the world's deepest lake. The Caspian Sea is the largest sea surrounded by land. The Volga River is the longest river in all of Europe. Look for these bodies of water on the map on pages four and five.

Brain Teaser

The Volga is not the longest river in Russia. The Volga is the longest river in Europe. How can this be? Remember that Russia covers parts of Europe and parts of Asia. Russia's longest river, the Lena, flows through Asian Russia.

Lake Baikal is more than a mile deep.

On the Move

Muscovites (the people of Moscow) are proud of their **subway** system. It is safe, clean, and cheap. But many Russians are buying cars. Bicyclists are seen outside Russia's cities, in the countryside.

One of the stops on the Moscow subway (left) will let you off near a big church called *St. Basil's Cathedral* (below on facing page).

Dear Nana

Mom and Dad took me on a long, long train ride. We even slept on the train. We mostly saw grass from the windows. We met some Russians on the train. All I could say in Russian was hello! I showed one Russian girl how to say hello in English. When we got to the end of the trip, Dad said we were near the Sea of Japan. He says Japan is not far away.

Love
Maddy

Sum Mainitian
Waum Kaillim
Thaluuhu, Simlu
730 n, Lauratu

People

Buryat women

(Below) *An older Russian*

Kids from Sakhalin Island

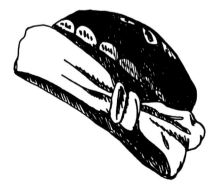

Ethnic Russian schoolgirls

Hundreds of **ethnic groups** live in Russia. The people of an ethnic group share a language, a religion, and a history. **Ethnic Russians** make up the biggest group in Russia. They are related to **Slavs,** who lived in the region thousands of years ago. Other peoples in Russia are the Tatars, the Chuvash, the Yakut, and the Buryat.

For special events, some Tatars put on colorful, old-style hats and dresses.

Most Russian kids live in cities. Some live in tall buildings called high-rises. What kind of home do you live in?

Home

Most Russians make their homes in the cities of European Russia. These cities include Moscow, the capital, or government center. St. Petersburg and Nizhni Novgorod are also big cities.

(Right) St. Petersburg is a big city on the Neva River. (Below) Russians who do not live in cities sometimes have to get their water from an outside pump.

Russian farmers do not live right next to their wheat or potato crops. They live in small villages and walk or ride to their fields every day.

Big paintings at a Soviet parade showed workers (left) *and the Soviet leader Vladimir Lenin* (below).

New Nation

For hundreds of years, leaders called czars ruled Russia. Then, in the year 1917, some Russians made the czar leave his palace.

These Russians formed a new nation called the Soviet Union. The Soviet Union was made up of Russia and many nearby countries.

In Russia these days a foodseller can raise or lower the prices for her fruit.

After 75 years, the Soviet Union fell apart. Russia was on its own again. Russian life changed. The people have more freedoms. But many Russians struggle to find jobs and to buy food.

Jobs

Finding a job in Russia is hard work. The country does not have enough jobs for everyone. Jobs are often easier to find in cities like Moscow and Nizhni Novgorod. Many of these workers make steel, cars, or chemicals.

Shoppers crowd the biggest street of Nizhni Novgorod.

Prices rise quickly in Russia. If you have enough rubles (Russian money) to buy five pencils on Monday, the same amount may buy you only four pencils by Friday!

Me next! People in Moscow line up to buy bread.

Some Russians are starting their own businesses. This is easier to do these days because Russians have more freedom.

21

Brothers clowning in Siberia

Family

In Russian families, both parents usually have to work. Russian men and women can hold the same jobs. They may be sellers, scientists, or soldiers. Russian women have a lot to do. After work, they come home to

Inside a one-room apartment

All in the Family

Here are the Russian words for some family members. Try them out on your own family!

father	atyets	(ah-TYETS)
mother	mat'	(MAHT)
uncle	dyadya	(DZYAH-dzyah)
aunt	tyotya	(TZYOH-tzyah)
grandfather	dyedushka	(DZYAH-doosh-kah)
grandmother	babushka	(BAH-boosh-kah)
son	sin	(SEHN)
daughter	doch'	(DOYCH)
brother	brat	(BRAHT)
sister	syestra	(seh-STRAH)

do housework and to take care of the children. Russian families often get help from their *babushka*, or grandmother.

The red soup called borscht and foods for a zakuska

Food

Russians love good food! A Russian dinner usually begins with a *zakuska*, a large plateful of easy-to-eat foods that everyone shares. A popular dinnertime soup, known as borscht, is bright red because of the beets that are in it. Another dinner dish, beef Stroganoff, puts together beef stew and noodles. *Kompot*, a sweet fruit drink, ends the meal.

Make Your Own Zakuska

Here are some ideas for putting together your own zakuska.
(Ask an older person to help you with the cutting.)

thinly sliced salami,
ham, cheeses, and radishes
cherry tomatoes, cut in half

cucumbers, peeled and sliced thin
dill pickles
bread rolls

Arrange the foods on a large platter. And remember, chatting about your day is a big part of enjoying a zakuska!

These Russians have just finished hunting for wild mushrooms.

This Pepsi sign is written in the Cyrillic alphabet. Which shape stands for P?

ABCs

The Russian alphabet, called **Cyrillic,** is much different from the Roman alphabet used for English. A man named Cyril, who lived about 1,000 years ago, made up the

If you meet a Russian . . .

Here are some good words to know.

IN ENGLISH	IN RUSSIAN
Yes	DAH
No	NYET
Hello	ZDRAH-stvwee-tyeh
Good-bye	dah-svee-DAHN-yah

alphabet. Only
Russian and a few
other languages
use it.

*This sign is selling American
hot dogs.*

A Russian lights a candle in a church.

Russian children enjoy Christmas with Father Frost.

Celebrate!

Russians celebrate many holidays. Some of them have to do with religion. Most people in Russia are either Russian Orthodox, Muslim, or Jewish. Each group honors different events. Easter is the most important holiday for Russian Orthodox Christians. Families feast throughout Easter week. Muslims pray a lot during the month of Ramadan and do not eat until the sun sets. On Yom Kippur, Jews pray for forgiveness of their sins.

St. Basil's Cathedral has nine colorful towers.

School

Most schools in
Russia are free.
Children in Russia
spend a lot of time

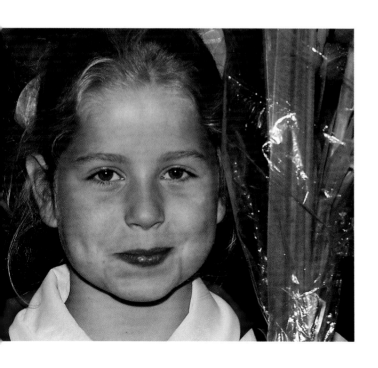

(Left) *This girl brings a flower for her teacher on the first day of school.* (Above) *A boy helps his brother read a book.*

After taking a hard test, some Russian students are allowed to go to Moscow University.

in the classroom. School bells ring six days a week, ten months a year. Students get grades of one, two, three, four, or five. Five is the highest mark. A three is a pretty good mark. Russian kids study reading, writing, math, science, history, and geography.

flute

oboe

French
horns

clarinet

bassoon

Story Time

Russian children enjoy stories set to music or dance. *The Nutcracker* and *Swan Lake* are popular ballets based on old stories. Folktales are also Russian favorites.

Peter and the Wolf has long been popular. A Russian named Sergey Prokofiev wrote the story's words and the music. Prokofiev wrote the music to teach children

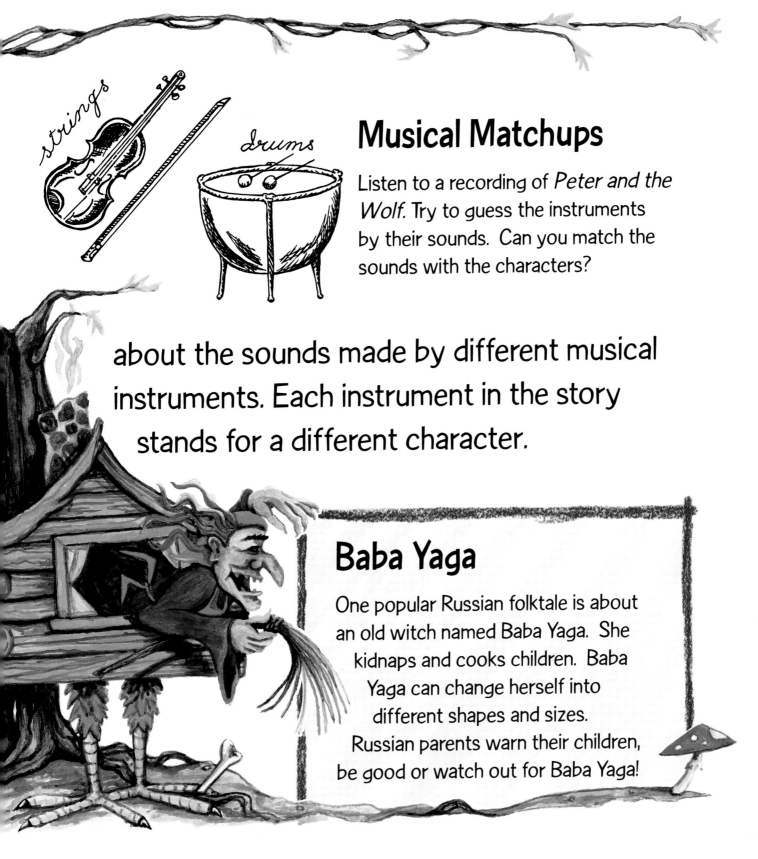

strings

drums

Musical Matchups

Listen to a recording of _Peter and the Wolf._ Try to guess the instruments by their sounds. Can you match the sounds with the characters?

about the sounds made by different musical instruments. Each instrument in the story stands for a different character.

Baba Yaga

One popular Russian folktale is about an old witch named Baba Yaga. She kidnaps and cooks children. Baba Yaga can change herself into different shapes and sizes. Russian parents warn their children, be good or watch out for Baba Yaga!

Ballet

Many talented ballet dancers are Russian. They often dance to music written by Russians. One of the most famous ballets is *The Nutcracker*, a Christmas story.

Mikhail Baryshnikov leaps during The Nutcracker. *What a jump!*

A Christmas Favorite

Tchaikovsky's ballet, *The Nutcracker,* has become a Christmastime favorite. Here's the story.

At Christmas, young Clara receives a wooden nutcracker for cracking open nuts. The nutcracker looks like a soldier. Later, after Clara goes to bed, she dreams that she is watching a battle take place between her toy soldiers and some mice. Her nutcracker fights the mouse king but must be rescued by Clara, who throws her shoe at the king. After the battle, the nutcracker is changed into a handsome prince. He leads Clara through the Land of Snowflakes to the Kingdom of Sweets. The kingdom's people, including the Sugar Plum Fairy, dance for the girl.

Peter Tchaikovsky, a Russian composer, wrote the music for the ballet.

Old-style Russian music almost always includes the sounds of a balalaika. A balalaika is a type of guitar with three strings. The Tatars created the balalaika a long time ago.

Music

Music is important to Russians. They love to sing folk songs at family gatherings. Just as meaningful are classical works such as *Peter*

Fans of Michael Jackson wait for him to come out of his hotel before a show.

and the *Wolf* and *The Nutcracker*. But if you turn on a radio in Russia, you are most likely to hear songs by Madonna and Michael Jackson.

Sports and Fun

Russians often win at worldwide sporting events. Russian athletes train hard. Most of their days are spent practicing. Soccer is a favorite sport in Russia. A team called the Moscow Spartak plays soccer against teams throughout Europe.

The race is on for these cross-country skiers!

Checkmate!

In school Russian children learn about czars and czarinas (the wives of czars). But in their time off, kids study kings and queens. These are playing pieces in chess. People play chess in parks throughout Russia. Thousands of Russian children are masters, or experts. The world chess champion is almost always a Russian.

Thanks to McDonald's and other American restaurants, Russians are getting a taste of American fast food.

New Words

The Russian language may look a lot different than English, but I will bet you already know some Russian words. How about *nyet?* Or *Sputnik?* Russians have added some American words to their language. *Biznesmen* means businessmen. Jeans are *jinzi*, and sneakers (Keds) are *kedi*.

Don't be fooled into thinking all Russians are like Boris and Natasha of The Rocky and Bullwinkle Show.

Beep. Beep. Beep.

This is the sound the first *Sputnik* made. What is a *Sputnik?* It is a spaceship the Soviet Union sent into space in 1957. A later Sputnik carried a dog named Laika. Laika was the world's very first space traveler.

TV

Television is becoming very popular in Russia. There are more programs than ever before.

Russians like to watch quiz shows, such as What? Where? When?

Viewers can watch news programs, game shows, talk shows, movies, sports, and foreign comedy shows. Young Russians enjoy *Ulitsa Sezam*—the Russian version of *Sesame Street.* Big Bird is blue and goes by the name of Zeliboba.

Russian families also watch the news together. On the screen is the Russian president, Boris Yeltsin.

New Words to Learn

Asian Russia: The eastern three-fourths of Russia that lies on the Asian continent.

continent: Any one of seven large areas of land. The continents are Africa, Antarctica, Asia, Australia, Europe, North America, and South America. Russia is on the continents of both Asia and Europe.

These small dolls carry the faces of famous Russian and Soviet leaders. Can you find President Yeltsin?

Cyrillic: An alphabet made for people who speak Slavic languages. A man named Cyril created the alphabet.

ethnic group: A group of people with many things, such as language and religion, in common.

ethnic Russian: A person from an early Slavic people called Russians. Ethnic Russians are the largest ethnic group in Russia.

European Russia: The western one-fourth of Russia that lies on the European continent.

Siberia: A huge region of Asian Russia.

Slav: A member of an ethnic group that came from central Asia and later moved into Russia and eastern Europe.

steppe: A flat plain that covers southern Russia.

subway: An underground train that moves large numbers of people quickly.

taiga: A large evergreen forest that goes from the Gulf of Finland in northwestern Russia to eastern Siberia.

tundra: A region where the soil is always frozen. The tundra stretches across the northernmost parts of Russia.

New Words to Say

Baikal	by-KAHL
balalaika	bah-luh-LY-kuh
borscht	BORSH
Buryat	bur-YAHT
Cyrillic	suh-RIH-lihk
czar	TSAHR
Nizhni Novgorod	NIZH-nee NAHV-guh-rahd
Prokofiev	pruh-KAWF-yehf
ruble	ROO-buhl
steppe	STEHP
Stroganoff	STRAW-guh-nawf
Tatar	TAH-tahr
Tchaikovsky	chy-KAWF-skee
Ulitsa Sezam	oo-LEE-tzah say-ZAHM
Ural	YUR-uhl
Yakut	yuh-KOOT
Yom Kippur	yohm kih-POOR
zakuska	zah-KOOS-kah
Zeliboba	zeh-lee-BOH-bah

More Books to Read

Arnold, Helen. *Russia.* Austin, TX: Raintree Steck-Vaughn Publishers, 1995.

Bickman, Connie. *Children of Russia.* Edina, MN: Abdo & Daughters, 1994.

Haskins, Jim. *Count Your Way through Russia.* Minneapolis: Carolrhoda Books, Inc., 1987.

Kendall, Russ. *Russian Girl: Life in an Old Russian Town.* New York: Scholastic, 1994.

Krasnopolsky, Fara L. *I Remember.* Boston: Houghton Mifflin Company, 1995.

Lye, Keith. *Passport to Russia.* Danbury, CT: Franklin Watts, Inc., 1996.

Morris, Ann. *Dancing to America.* New York: Dutton, 1994.

Nottingham, Ted. *Chess for Children.* New York: Sterling Publishing Company, 1996.

Plotkin, Gregory, and Ruth Plotkin. *Cooking the Russian Way.* Minneapolis: Lerner Publications Company, 1986.

Polacco, Patricia. *Babushka Baba Yaga.* New York: Putnam Publishing Group, 1993.

New Words to Find

Asian Russia, 5, 6, 11

ballet, 32, 34–35

Caspian Sea, 10–11
czars, 18, 39

European Russia, 5, 16

families, 22–23
farmers, 10, 17
food, 19, 24–25
forests, 7, 8, 9

games, 39, 42

holidays, 28–29
homes, 16–17, 22

jobs, 7, 20–21, 22

language, 23, 26–27, 40–41

map of Russia, 4–5
Moscow, 13, 16, 20, 21
mountains, 5, 8
music, 32–33, 34–35, 36–37

people, 14–15

religion, 28–29
rivers and lakes, 9, 10–11, 17

schools, 30–31, 39
Siberia, 6, 10
Soviet Union, 19, 41
sports, 38
steppes, 8–9
storytelling, 32–33, 35

television, 42–43
travel methods, 6, 12–13
tundra, 6–7